11+
Maths

Numerical Reasoning
Standard & Multiple-choice 6 Minute Tests

TESTBOOK 3

Dr Stephen C Curran

Edited by Andrea Richardson

This book belongs to

Accelerated Education Publications Ltd.

Do your workings on this page

Mark to %	
0	0%
1	17%
2	33%
3	50%
4	67%
5	83%
6	100%

Daily Test 1

1) What is the missing number? _____

49	65	81
65	81	97
81	97	

2) Look at the diagram below:

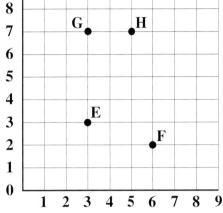

What are the co-ordinates of the points at letter **F** and letter **G**?

F: (____ , ____)

G: (____ , ____)

3) Jim's father is now **3** times as old as Jim was **5** years ago.

If Jim's father is **45**, how old is Jim?

_____

4) Which of these sets of numbers contains all square numbers?

A **16 36 56**
B **46 49 72**
C **36 64 90**
D **36 49 144**
E **72 120 144** _____

5) Look at the Venn diagram below.

It shows how many children in Miss Roger's class play tennis, rounders or both. **4** children play neither.

There are **36** children in the class.

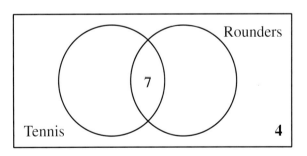

If **18** children play tennis, how many children in the class play rounders?

_____

6) Find the missing number so that the equation balances.

$$64 \div 8 \times 3 = 39 \div 3 + \underline{}$$

Score [   ] Percentage [   ] %

Do your workings on this page

Mark to %	
0	0%
1	17%
2	33%
3	50%
4	67%
5	83%
6	100%

Daily Test 2

1) Jacqueline has **three** 50 pence pieces, **four** 20 pence pieces, **three** 10 pence pieces and **one** 5 pence piece in her pocket.

How much money does she have in total? _____

---

2) This is a map of the tunnels under Vernon Castle.
Find the way from the Kitchen to the Lounge using a set of instructions.

Key:
FD means forward, **RT** means turn right **90°** and **LT** means turn left **90°**.

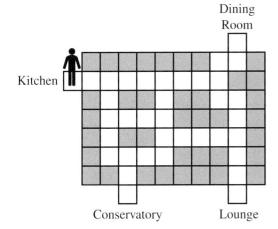

Which of these sets of instructions is the correct one?

A FD 5, RT, FD 3, RT, FD 4, RT, FD 3.

B FD 8 , LT, FD 5, LT, FD 2, RT, FD 6.

C FD 2, LT, FD 3, RT, FD 5, RT, FD 3.

D FD 5, RT, FD 3, LT, FD 4, RT, FD 3.

E FD 2, RT, FD 3, LT, FD 8, RT, FD 6.

_____

---

3) There are **16** mini chocolate bars in a packet.

How many packets would **336** bars fill? _____

4) Jenny works as a waitress. In the last four days she has received the following tips:
£2.75, **£3.55**, **£4.65** and **£3.95**.

How much are the tips worth in total?

_____

5) This graph shows the conversion rate between UK pounds (£) and US dollars ($).

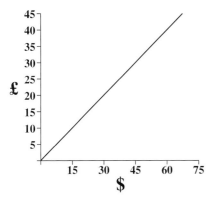

How many dollars need to be exchanged to get **£30**? _____

6) Ayleston Rovers Juniors played the Wickan Rangers Juniors in a football match. The match kicked off at **2.15pm**. They played **35** minutes each half and had a half-time break of **10** minutes.

At what time in 12-hour clock did the match end? _____

Score ☐ Percentage ☐

Do your workings on this page

Mark to %	
0	0%
1	17%
2	33%
3	50%
4	67%
5	83%
6	100%

Daily Test 3

1) Look at the net. When folded it makes a box. If the side of each small square is **2cm**, what will be the total surface area of the box?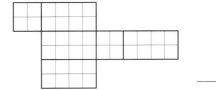

_____

2) There are **36** children on a bus; **20** girls and **16** boys. **One** child's name is chosen at random to collect the tickets.

What is the chance that the child will be a girl?

(Give the answer as a fraction in its lowest terms.)

_____

3) **120** children took part in a *Guess the weight of the box of sweets* competition.

$\frac{5}{8}$ guessed too high. $\frac{1}{4}$ guessed too low.

How many children guessed the correct weight of the box of sweets?

_____

4) This is Geoff's function machine.

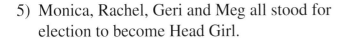

$? \longrightarrow$ Divide by **4** $\longrightarrow$ Add **10** $\longrightarrow 25$

What number did he start with?

_____

5) Monica, Rachel, Geri and Meg all stood for election to become Head Girl.

200 children in the school voted for which girl they wanted to be the Head Girl.

The percentages of votes cast are shown in the pie chart.

How many votes did Rachel receive?

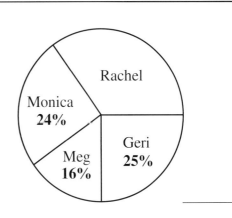

_____

6) How would **10.30 in the evening** be written as a time on a 24-hour clock?

_____

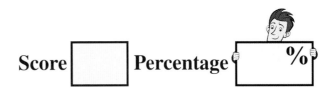

Score [ ] Percentage [ ] %

Do your workings on this page

Mark to %	
0	0%
1	17%
2	33%
3	50%
4	67%
5	83%
6	100%

Daily Test 4

1) **Five** children spend their weekend delivering leaflets advertising the school fête. The bar chart below shows how many each of the children delivered.

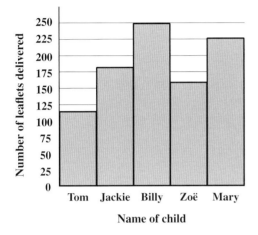

How many more leaflets were delivered by Mary than by Tom?

_____

2) Mr and Mrs Bridge take their **three** children to the circus. Tickets cost **£3.75** each for children. The price of an adult's ticket is **£2.50** more than that of a child.

How much does it cost the family to visit the circus?

_____

3) How many faces does a triangular prism have? _____

4) The ratio of flour to sugar in a cake is **5 : 3**.

If **600g** of sugar is used to make the cake, how many kilograms of flour are used? _____

5) This spinner has an equal chance of landing on any of the numbers.

What is the chance that it will come to rest on a number that is a multiple of **7**?

Write the answer as a fraction in its lowest possible terms.

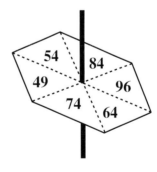

_____

6) The hands of the classroom clock show the time **5 o'clock**.

What is the smaller angle between the hour hand and the minute hand?

_____

Score [   ] Percentage [**%**]

Do your workings on this page

Mark to %	
0	0%
1	17%
2	33%
3	50%
4	67%
5	83%
6	100%

Daily Test 5

1) Jenny places some weights on an electronic scale. She needs to make a total of **5.3kg**.

Which two of the weights below should she choose to make up the weight to the correct amount?

A **375g**
B **275g**
C **225g**
D **325g**
E **350g**

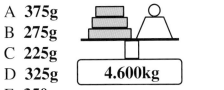

4.600kg

_____ and _____

2) Helen and Ian go to an athletics club after school each weekday during the summer term. They each have to pay **70p** a day to attend.

Helen pays an extra **30p** a day to have a shower afterwards but Ian waits until he gets home.

How much will it cost the pair of them to go to the athletics club for **one** week?

_____

3)

Paddington   Edgware Road   Marylebone   Baker Street

A London Underground train ran between Paddington and Baker Street stations. There were **45** passengers on the train when it left Paddington. **7** people got out at Edgware Road and **16** people got on. **18** left the train at Marylebone whilst **25** got on.

How many people were on the train when it arrived at Baker Street? _____

4) Eric spends **y** pounds each day on chewing gum. He spends **x** pounds each week on soft drinks.

How much does Eric spend altogether in **one** week?

A **5x + 2y**
B **7x + 7y**
C **2x + 5y**
D **7x + y**
E **x + 7y**

_____

5) The area of the shaded part of this shape is **35cm²**.

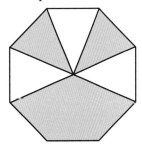

What is the area of the whole shape? _____

6) Mr Bonner bought **294** small daffodil bulbs for the school garden. They come packed in boxes of **14**.

How many boxes of bulbs did Mr Bonner buy? _____

Score [   ] Percentage [%]

Do your workings on this page

Mark to %	
0	0%
1	17%
2	33%
3	50%
4	67%
5	83%
6	100%

Daily Test 6

1) At the end of January there were **765** litres of oil in a tank.

   168 litres were used in February.
   148 litres were used in March.

   How many litres remain unused?

   _____

2) This is a floor plan of the school dining room.

   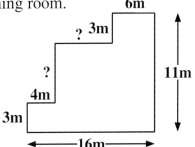

   What is the total perimeter of the floor? _____

3) Michelle is flying to Moscow in Russia to visit her pen friend, Ludmilla. There is a time difference between the United Kingdom and Moscow. Michelle's home in London is **4** hours behind Ludmilla's home in Moscow. It takes **4** hours to fly from London to Moscow.

   If Michelle's plane leaves London at **11am**, what will the time be in Moscow when her plane touches down? (Remember to state am or pm.) _____

4) What fraction of an hour is **40** minutes?

   Write the answer in its lowest possible terms. _____

5) The product of two numbers is **72**. The difference between the two numbers is **6**.

   What are the two numbers?

   _____ and _____

6) Look carefully at this graph.

   What is the rule that governs the plotting of Line A?

   A $y + 2 = x$
   B $y - 2 = x$
   C $2x = y + 4$
   D $x + 1 = y$
   E $2x = y$

   _____

   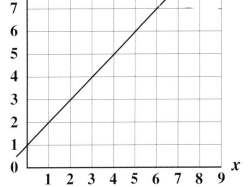

   Score [ ]   Percentage [%]

Do your workings on this page

Mark to %	
0	0%
1	17%
2	33%
3	50%
4	67%
5	83%
6	100%

Daily Test 7

1) The local computer shop has a sale.
Every item in the shop is reduced by **25%**.
Bobby buys a game for his computer.
It normally costs **£28.00**.

How much does Bobby have to
pay for the game in the sale? _____

3) Which of the figures below shows the
number **thirty-three thousand and three**?

A **33,303**

B **3,330,03**

C **33,003**

D **3,303**

E **330,003** _____

2) Look carefully at the grid below.

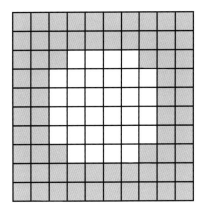

What percentage of
this grid has been shaded?

_____

4) This half-term Nicola has taken **7** times tables tests. Here are her results out of **20**:

14 11 8 16 15 17 10

What was her mean score? _____

5) Look at the number line.

What is the value of the
number that the arrow is
pointing to? _____

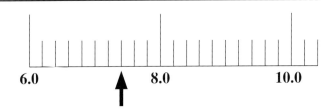

6) Mrs Campbell's class did a survey in their school on favourite sports
television programmes.

Favourite TV Programmes	
World Cup Cricket	☐■
Sunday Athletics	☐☐
Olympic Special	☐☐☐■
World Ice Skating	☐☐■
FA Cup Football	☐☐☐☐■

Key:

☐ **6 children**

■ **3 children**

How many children liked
the Olympic Special show?

_____

Score ☐ Percentage ☐ **%**

Do your workings on this page

Mark to %	
0	0%
1	17%
2	33%
3	50%
4	67%
5	83%
6	100%

Daily Test 8

1) Neil and Caroline went to the local shop to buy some party hats for a Christmas party. In the shop there were five different packs at five different prices:

   A Special Paper   £3.80 / pack of **10**
   B Santa Hats   £4.50 / pack of **15**
   C Multicoloured   £4.40 / pack of **20**
   D Assorted   £7.50 / pack of **25**
   E Shiny Silver   £6.00 / pack of **12**

   Which pack contains the hats at the lowest individual price? _____

---

2) Rachel, Zoë, Robert and Thomas all stood for election to the school council.

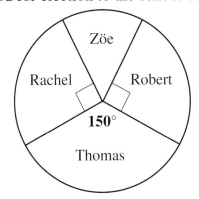

   180 children in the school voted for which child they wanted to be their representative on the council.

   How many votes did Zoë receive? _____

3) If **5y + 10 = 25**, what is the value of **y**? _____

4) Francine, Barbara, Melanie, Justine and Claire each bought a CD from the local music shop.

   Francine paid **£7.99**, Melanie paid **£8.50**, Barbara paid **£12.95**, Claire paid **£10.99** and Justine paid **£9.50**.

   What was the range of the prices paid? _____

---

5) Which of these shapes has a rotational symmetry of order **1**?

   A   B   C   D   E

---

6) Mervyn's dad takes Mervyn and his three friends to the pantomime for a treat. It costs **£9.00** each for adults and **£5.00** each for children. Each child also bought an ice cream and Mervyn's dad had a cup of coffee. Ice creams cost **£1.25** each and a cup of coffee costs **£1.60**.

   How much did the trip cost Mervyn's dad altogether? _____

   Score [   ]   Percentage [   ] %

Do your workings on this page

Mark to %	
0	0%
1	17%
2	33%
3	50%
4	67%
5	83%
6	100%

Daily Test 9

1) Look at the nets below.

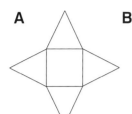 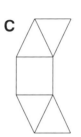 

A   B   C   D   E

Which of these nets will fold to form a
triangular-based pyramid?

_____ and _____

2) Colleen and Sinita go to the homework club each weekday evening during
the summer term. They each have to pay **80p** a day to attend. Sinita pays an
extra **30p** a day for a drink but Colleen takes her own.

How much will it cost the pair of them to go to the homework club
for **one** week?

_____

3) Sam's mum buys **four 3** litre
bottles of cola from the
supermarket.

Approximately how much do the
four bottles weigh altogether?

Give the answer in kilograms.

_____

4) This is a magic square.
All the columns, rows and diagonals
add up to **45**.

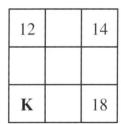

12		14
K		18

What is the
value of **K**?

_____

5) Jane places **9** balls into a black bag. **Two** are red, **four** are blue and **three** are yellow.
She takes **one** ball at random from the bag and places it on the table. It is yellow.

What is the chance that the next ball out of the bag will be red?

A $\frac{2}{9}$ B $\frac{1}{4}$ C $\frac{3}{8}$ D $\frac{1}{3}$ E $\frac{1}{6}$

_____

6) Which of the following numbers has a value closest to **10**?

9.995 10.899 10.190 9.909 9.992

_____

Score [ ] Percentage [%]

Do your workings on this page

2016 Stephen Curran ae

Mark to %	
0	0%
1	17%
2	33%
3	50%
4	67%
5	83%
6	100%

Daily Test 10

1) Three corners of a rectangle have the co-ordinates (**6**, **6**), (**1**, **2**) and (**1**, **6**).

What are the co-ordinates of the fourth corner?   (____ , ____)

---

2) Which of these shapes contains one obtuse angle?

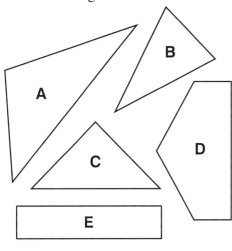

_____

3) What is the total area of the triangle?

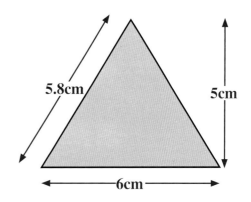

5.8cm   5cm

6cm

_____

---

4) Look at the graph.

What are the co-ordinates of **P** and **Q**?

	P	**Q**
A	(-2, -3)	(4, 1)
B	(-2, -1)	(1, 4)
C	(-3, 2)	(3, 1)
D	(-3, -2)	(1, 4)
E	(2, -3)	(4, 1)

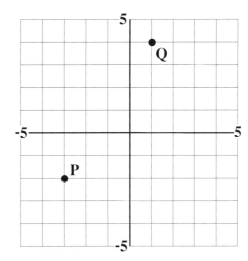

_____

---

5) What is **10.7561** rounded to 2 decimal places?

_____

6) Complete the following sequence:

5, 15, 35, 45, 65, ____

Score [   ] Percentage [%]

Do your workings on this page

Mark to %	
0	0%
1	17%
2	33%
3	50%
4	67%
5	83%
6	100%

Daily Test 11

1) Drew spends x pounds each week on sweets. He spends y pounds each month on magazines.

How much does Drew spend altogether in **one** year?

A $52x + 12y$
B $12x + 7y$
C $52x + 5y$
D $7x + 52y$
E $12x + 52y$ _____

2) The shaded area of the shape below is **35cm²**.

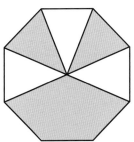

What is the area of the unshaded part? _____

3) Mr Jennings bought **342** party hats for the school Christmas party. They are packed in boxes of **18**.

How many boxes of party hats did Mr Jennings buy? _____

4) Taylor places some weights on an electronic scale. She needs to make a total of **5.8kg**.

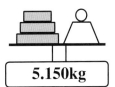

5.150kg

Which two of the weights below should she choose to make up the weight to the correct amount?

A **325g**
B **275g**
C **225g**
D **375g**
E **350g**   _____ and _____

5) Simone and Barry go to the burger bar each weekday during half term week. They each pay **£1.20** for a burger. They spend an extra **90p** a day for some fries, which they share.

How much does it cost the pair of them to go to the burger bar during the week? _____

Waterloo   Embankment   Charing Cross   Piccadilly Circus

6) A London Underground train ran between Waterloo and Piccadilly Circus stations. There were **50** passengers on the train when it left Waterloo. **27** people got out at Embankment and **14** people got on. **8** people left the train at Charing Cross while **25** people got on.

How many people were on the train at Piccadilly Circus? _____

Score [ ] Percentage [%]

Do your workings on this page

Mark to %	
0	0%
1	17%
2	33%
3	50%
4	67%
5	83%
6	100%

Daily Test 12

1) The ratio of pasta to sauce in a lasagne recipe is **5 : 3**.

   If **450g** of sauce was used, how much pasta was used? _____

2) This spinner has an equal chance of landing on any of the numbers.

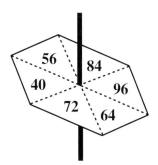

   What is the chance that it will come to rest on a number that is a multiple of **6**?

   Write the answer as a fraction in its lowest possible terms. _____

3) The hands of the classroom clock show the time **4 o'clock**.

   What is the reflex angle between the hour hand and the minute hand? _____

4) Mrs Davis keeps a record of all cakes sold in the school canteen in a week. This bar chart shows how many cakes were sold in a particular week.

   How many more cakes were bought on Wednesday than on Monday? _____

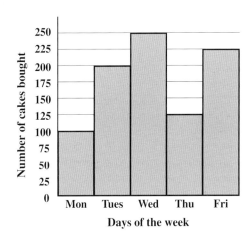

5) Mr and Mrs Jackson take their four children to a rugby match. Tickets cost **£7.50** each for adults. The price of a child's ticket is **£2.75** less than that of an adult.

   How much does it cost the family to attend the rugby match? _____

6) How many faces does a dodecahedron have? _____

Score [ ] Percentage [%]

Do your workings on this page

Mark to %	
0	0%
1	17%
2	33%
3	50%
4	67%
5	83%
6	100%

Daily Test 13

1) This is Jenny's function machine.

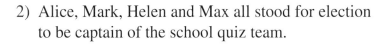

? ⟶ Divide by **5** ⟶ Subtract **10** ⟶ 5

   What number did she start with? _____

---

2) Alice, Mark, Helen and Max all stood for election to be captain of the school quiz team.

   200 children in the school voted for which pupil they wanted to be the captain. The percentages of votes cast are shown in the pie chart.

   How many votes did Alice receive? _____

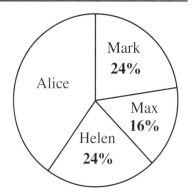

---

3) How should **11.30 at night** be written as a time on a 24-hour clock? _____

---

4) Look at the net below. When folded it makes a box.

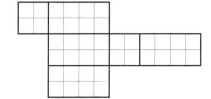

   If each small square has an area of **5cm²**, what is the total surface area of the box? _____

---

5) There are **48** children on a train; **16** girls and **32** boys.
   One child's name is chosen at random to collect the tickets.

   What is the chance that the child will be a boy?
   (Give the answer as a fraction in its lowest terms.) _____

---

6) **180** children took part in a *Guess the teacher's age* competition.

   $\frac{5}{9}$ guessed too high and $\frac{1}{4}$ guessed too low.

   How many children guessed the correct age of the teacher? _____

Score [   ] Percentage [   ] %

Do your workings on this page

Mark to %	
0	0%
1	17%
2	33%
3	50%
4	67%
5	83%
6	100%

Daily Test 14

1) Jenny has the job of totalling the money collected in some charity tins.
Today she has four tins to check. They contain **£1.99**, **£7.63**, **£14.65** and **£8.93**.

How much was collected in all four tins? _____

2) This graph shows the conversion rate between Swiss francs (f) and UK pounds (£).

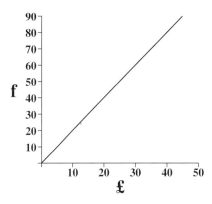

How many pounds would need to be exchanged to make **f80**? _____

3) Ufton Junior played Smithton Primary in a football match.

The match kicked off at **2.20pm**. They played **25** minutes each half, and had a half-time break of **20** minutes.

At what time did the match end? _____

4) Leonora has **five** 50 pence pieces, **two** 20 pence pieces, **one** ten pence piece and **two** 5 pence pieces in her pocket.

How much money does she have in total? _____

5) This is a map of the tunnels under Morton Castle. Find the way from the Dining Room to the Lounge using a set of instructions.

Key:
FD means forward, **RT** means turn right **90°** and **LT** means turn left **90°**.

Which of these sets of instructions is the correct one?

A FD 6, LT, FD 3, LT, FD 4, RT, FD 3.
B FD 6, RT, FD 4, RT, FD 3, LT, FD 4.
C FD 6, RT, FD 3, LT, FD 4, RT, FD 3.
D FD 6, RT, FD 3, RT, FD 4, LT, FD 3.
E FD 5, RT, FD 3, RT, FD 5, LT, FD 3.

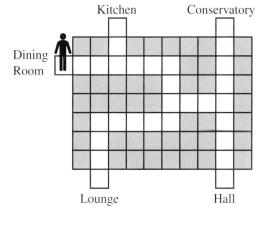

_____

6) Bob's mother is now **4** times as old as Bob was **2** years ago.

If Bob is **9**, how old is his mother? _____

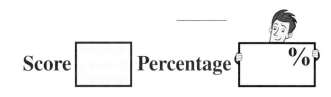

Score ____ Percentage ____ %

Do your workings on this page

© 2016 Stephen Curran

Mark to %	
0	0%
1	17%
2	33%
3	50%
4	67%
5	83%
6	100%

Daily Test 15

1) Which of these sets of numbers contains all square numbers?

   A **4**, **9**, **18**
   B **12**, **16**, **35**
   C **18**, **27**, **64**
   D **16**, **36**, **81**
   E **25**, **99**, **121**   _____

2) Look at the Venn diagram below. It shows how many children in Mrs Blade's class like sausages, mashed potato or both. **4** children like neither. There are **32** children in the class. Some numbers are missing.

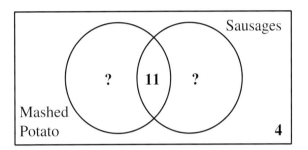

3) Find the missing number so that the equation balances.

   $4 \times 8 + 20 = 5 \times 5 +$ ____

4)

13	26	39
26	39	52
39	52	

   What is the missing number?   _____

   If **23** children like mashed potato and **16** like sausages, how many children in the class like only mashed potato?

   _____

5) Look at the diagram.

   What are the co-ordinates of the points at letter **W** and letter **X**?

   W: (____ , ____)

   X: (____ , ____)

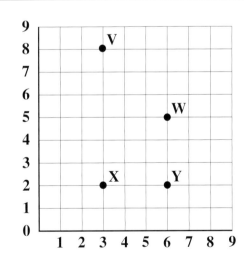

6) There are **12** fairy cakes in a packet.

   How many packets would **372** cakes fill?   _____

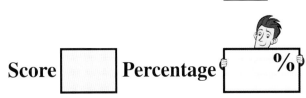

Score ☐   Percentage ☐ %

Do your workings on this page

Mark to %	
0	0%
1	17%
2	33%
3	50%
4	67%
5	83%
6	100%

Daily Test 16

1) Look at the graph to the right.

   What are the co-ordinates of **F** and **G**?

	F	**G**
A	(-2, 1)	(3, 2)
B	(-3, 2)	(1, -2)
C	(-3, -2)	(2, -1)
D	(1, -2)	(-2, 3)
E	(-3, 2)	(-1, -2)

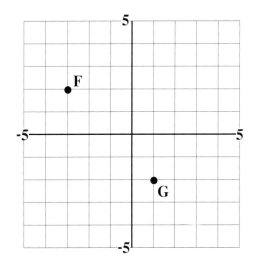

   _____

---

2) What is **59.095** to 1 decimal place?

   _____

3) Complete the following sequence:

   7, 14, 22, 31, 41, ____

---

4) Three corners of a rectangle have the co-ordinates (**3, 2**), (**5, 9**) and (**3, 9**).

   What are the co-ordinates of the fourth corner?   (____ , ____)

---

5) Which one of these shapes has only one obtuse angle?

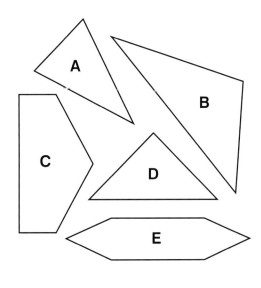

   _____

6) What is the total area of this parallelogram?

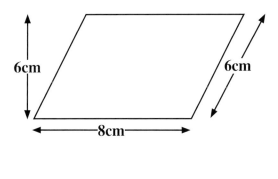

   _____

Score [____]   Percentage [____] %

Do your workings on this page

Mark to %	
0	0%
1	17%
2	33%
3	50%
4	67%
5	83%
6	100%

Daily Test 17

21		19
	P	15

1) All the columns, rows and diagonals add up to **54**.

   What is the value of **P**?

   _____

2) Rebecca places **10** balls into a black bag. **Three** are red, **two** are green and **five** are blue. She takes **one** ball at random from the bag and places it on the table. It is blue.

   What is the chance that the next ball out of the bag will be another blue?

   A $\frac{4}{9}$ B $\frac{5}{9}$ C $\frac{3}{8}$ D $\frac{1}{2}$ E $\frac{3}{7}$

   _____

3) Catherine and Alex go to Holiday Club each weekday morning during the summer. They each have to pay **£1.60** a day to attend. Alex pays an extra **40p** a day for a drink but Catherine takes her own.

   How much will it cost the pair of them to go to Holiday Club for **one** week?

   _____

4) Which one of these nets will not fold to form a triangular prism?

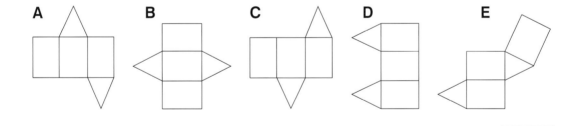

   _____

5) Which of the following numbers has a value closest to **100**?

   A **100.089**
   B **99.898**
   C **99.982**
   D **100.099**
   E **99.098**

   _____

6) Freda's dad buys **five 6** litre bottles of spring water from the supermarket.

   Approximately how much do they weigh altogether in kilograms?

   _____

Score [ ] Percentage [%]

Do your workings on this page

Mark to %	
0	0%
1	17%
2	33%
3	50%
4	67%
5	83%
6	100%

Daily Test 18

1) James, Sally, Kathryn, Rory and Cheryl each bought a computer game from the local shop.

James paid **£15.00**, Kathryn paid **£16.30**, Rory paid **£11.95**, Cheryl paid **£8.95** and Sally paid **£9.50**.

What was the range of the prices paid?

_____

2) Which of these shapes has a rotational symmetry of order **4**?

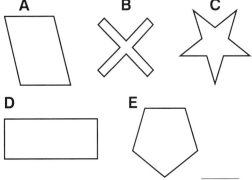

_____

3) Rachel's uncle takes Rachel and her two friends to Paris for a treat.
It costs **£54.00** each for adults and **£28.00** each for children.
They each have lunch on the train.
Lunches cost **£5.00** per person.

How much did the trip cost Rachel's uncle altogether?

_____

4) Sammy and Rebecca went to the local shop to buy some crackers for a Christmas party.
In the shop there were five different packs at five different prices:

A Big Bang crackers   **£3.45** / pack of **10**
B Reindeer Red crackers **£2.40** / pack of **8**
C Santa Special crackers **£4.80** / pack of **20**
D Magic Elf crackers   **£7.50** / pack of **25**
E Standard crackers   **£3.20** / pack of **16**

Which pack contains the crackers at the lowest individual price?   _____

5) Billy, Françoise, Jamal and Zoë all collected money for a disaster appeal.

Between them they collected **£600**. They drew a pie chart to show how much each of them had collected.

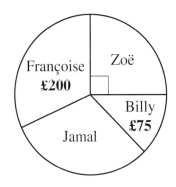

How much did Jamal collect?

_____

6) If **4x + 8 = 32**, what is the value of **x**?

_____

Score ☐ Percentage ☐ **%**

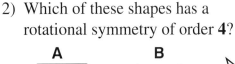

Do your workings on this page

Mark to %	
0	0%
1	17%
2	33%
3	50%
4	67%
5	83%
6	100%

Daily Test 19

1) This half-term Saeeda has taken **7** times tables tests.

Here are her results out of **20**:

16   13   19   15   12   18   12

What is her mean score?

_____

2) Look at the number line below

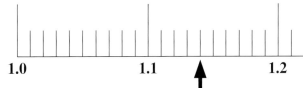

What is the value of the number that the arrow is pointing to?

_____

3) Mrs Campbell's class conducted a survey in their school on favourite ice creams.

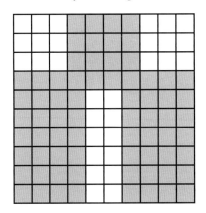

Favourite Ice Creams	
Raspberry Ripple	☐ ■ ■ ■
Cornish Vanilla	☐ ☐ ■
Chocolate Fudge	☐ ☐ ☐ ■ ■ ■
Peanut Surprise	☐ ☐ ■
Choc'n'mint	☐ ☐ ☐ ■ ■

Key:

☐ **5** children

■ **1** child

How many children liked the Choc'n'mint flavour?

_____

4) The local furniture shop has a sale.
Every item in the shop is reduced by **25%**.
Mrs Sibley buys a new sofa for her sitting room.
It normally costs **£360**.

How much does Mrs Sibley have to pay for the sofa in the sale? _____

5) Look carefully at the grid below.

What percentage of this grid has been shaded? _____

6) Which of the figures below shows the number **sixty-six thousand and sixteen**?

A **660,016**
B **60,616**
C **66,016**
D **66,160**
E **6,616**

_____

Score ☐   Percentage ☐ **%**

Do your workings on this page

© 2016 Stephen Curran

Mark to %	
0	0%
1	17%
2	33%
3	50%
4	67%
5	83%
6	100%

Daily Test 20

1) What fraction of a day is **18** hours?

   Write the answer in its lowest possible terms.

   _____

2) The product of two numbers is **45**. The difference between the two numbers is **12**.

   What are the two numbers?

   _____ and _____

3) Look carefully at the graph. What is the rule that governs the plotting of Line A?

   A $x = y - 4$
   B $x = y + 8$
   C $2x = y + 2$
   D $x + 5 = y$
   E $2x + 2 = y$

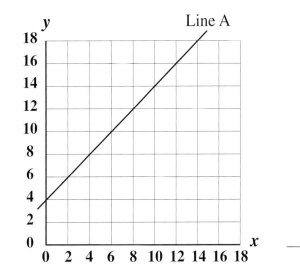

_____

4) In a factory there are **900** boxes of CDs. **238** are sold to high street music shops. **123** are sold to internet shops.

   How many boxes remain unsold?

   _____

5) This is a floor plan of the school dining room.

   What is the total perimeter of the floor?

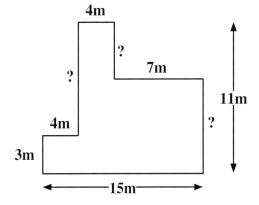

   _____

6) Geraldine is flying to Florida for a holiday with her family. She is looking forward to visiting the theme parks.

   There is a time difference between the United Kingdom and Florida in the United States. Geraldine's home in London is **5** hours ahead of Florida. It takes **9** hours to fly from London to Florida.

   If Geraldine's plane leaves London at **10am**, what will the time be in Florida when her plane touches down? (Remember to state am or pm.) _____

Score [ ] Percentage [%]

Do your workings on this page

© 2016 Stephen Curran

Mark to %	
0	0%
1	17%
2	33%
3	50%
4	67%
5	83%
6	100%

Daily Test 21

1) Sonia places some weights on an electronic scale.
She needs to make a total of **4.90kg**.

Which **two** of the weights below should she choose to make up the weight to the correct amount?

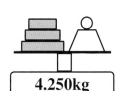

4.250kg

A **275g**
B **325g**
C **225g**
D **375g**
E **250g**

_____ and _____

2) Simone and Becky go to their grandmother's house on the bus each weekday during half term week.

The return journey on the bus costs them **£2.40** each.

Each day on the way home they also spend **£1.80** on some chips, from the fish and chip shop, which they share.

How much money does their mum have to give them to pay for everything during the week? _____

| Northampton | Long Buckley | Rugby | Coventry |

3) A train ran between Northampton and Coventry stations.
There were **60** passengers on the train when it left Northampton.
9 people got out at Long Buckley and **17** people got on.
Half the passengers left the train at Rugby while another **25** got on.

How many people were on the train when it arrived at Coventry? _____

4) Eric spends **x** pounds each day on bus fares. He spends **y** pounds each week on train fares.

How much does Eric spend altogether in a fortnight?

A **2y + 7x**
B **2x + 14y**
C **y + 14x**
D **7x + 2y**
E **14x + 2y**

_____

5) This shape is made up of **8** identical triangles.
This shaded part has an area of **125cm²**.

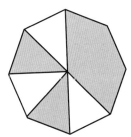

What is the area of the unshaded part? _____

6) Mrs Johnson bought **720** badges to sell in her shop.
They come packed in boxes of **48**.

How many boxes of badges did Mrs Johnson buy? _____

Score [ ] Percentage [%]

ae © 2016 Stephen Curran   43

Do your workings on this page

Mark to %	
0	0%
1	17%
2	33%
3	50%
4	67%
5	83%
6	100%

Daily Test 22

1) The ratio of flour to sugar in a recipe is **7 : 3**.

   If **150g** of sugar was used for the recipe, how much flour was used?

   _____

2) The spinner shown below has an equal chance of landing on any of the numbers.

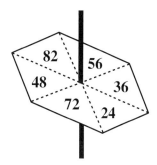

   What is the chance that it will come to rest on a number that is a multiple of both **3** and **4**?

   Write the answer as a fraction in its lowest possible terms.

   _____

3) The hands of the classroom clock show the time **2 o'clock**.

   What is the acute angle between the hour hand and the minute hand?

   _____

4) During the summer months the local council send a water truck around the area to spray water on the flowerbeds set in the middle of roundabouts. The bar chart shows how many litres of water were used in a particular week.

   How many more litres were used on Thursday than on Tuesday?

   _____

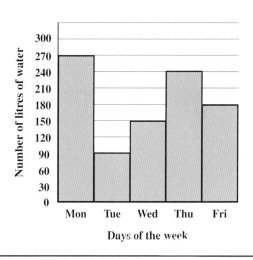

5) Mr and Mrs Hendry take their **three** children to a football match. Tickets cost **£11.00** each for adults. The price of a child's ticket is half that of an adult ticket.

   How much does it cost the family to attend the match?

   _____

6) How many faces are there on **three** hexahedrons?

   _____

Score [   ]   Percentage [   ] %

Do your workings on this page

Mark to %	
0	0%
1	17%
2	33%
3	50%
4	67%
5	83%
6	100%

Daily Test 23

1) This is Miya's function machine. What number did she start with?

$? \longrightarrow$ | Divide by **6** | $\longrightarrow$ | Subtract **14** | $\longrightarrow$ **6**

_____

2) Mr Williams' class took a survey of the main courses eaten by **120** children in the school canteen one lunchtime.

They counted up the numbers of different meals eaten and recorded the information on a pie chart.

How many children had mince and rice for lunch?

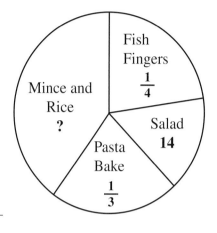

_____

3) How would **a quarter to two in the afternoon** be shown as a time on a 24-hour clock?

_____

4) Look at the net below.
When folded it makes a box.

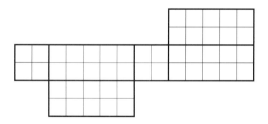

If the side of each small square is **5cm**, what will be the total volume of the box?

_____

5) There are **32** children in Mr Simmonds' class; **12** girls and **20** boys.

One child's name is chosen at random to collect the homework on Monday morning.

What is the chance that the child will be a girl?

(Write the answer as a fraction in its lowest terms.)

_____

6) **150** children took part in a *Guess the age of the head teacher* competition to raise money for charity.

50 guessed too high and **84** guessed too low.

How many children correctly guessed the head teacher's age?

_____

Score [ ] Percentage [%]

Do your workings on this page

Mark to %	
0	0%
1	17%
2	33%
3	50%
4	67%
5	83%
6	100%

Daily Test 24

1) Laura has **seven** 50 pence pieces, **one** 20 pence piece, **two** 10 pence pieces and **five** 5 pence pieces in her purse.

   How much money does she have in total? _____

---

2) This is a map of the classrooms in St George's school. Find the way from Mrs Smith's class to Mr Monkton's class using a set of instructions.

   Key:
   FD means forward, **RT** means turn right **90°**, **LT** means turn left **90°**.

   A FD 5, RT, FD2, LT, FD 4, LT, FD 4.
   B FD 6, RT, FD 3, LT, FD 4, RT, FD 3.
   C FD 5, LT, FD 2, RT, FD 4, RT, FD 4.
   D FD 6, RT, FD 2, LT, FD 4, RT, FD 3.
   E FD 5, RT, FD 3, RT, FD 4, LT, FD 4.

   _____

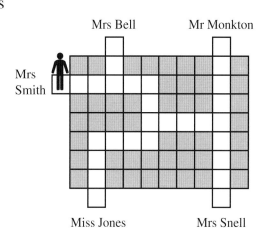

3) Jane's mother is now **twice** as old as Jane will be in **9** years' time.

   If Jane is **8** now, how old is her mother? _____

4) Ahmed had the job of totalling the money made on five stalls at the summer fair. In the five tins he found **£7.20**, **£8.40**, **£7.60**, **£11.50** and **£5.30**.

   How much did the five stalls make in total? _____

5) This graph shows the conversion rate between Japanese yen (¥) and UK pounds (£).

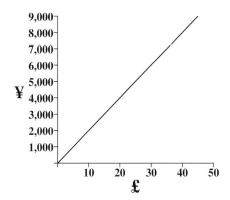

   How many pounds would need to be exchanged to make ¥8,000? _____

6) Smithton primary school went on a school trip to the sea. The coach set off at **8.30am** and drove for **1** hour **50** minutes before stopping for **20** minutes for a comfort break. After another **1** hour **30** minutes they arrived at the seaside.

   At what time did they arrive in 12-hour clock? _____

Score ☐ Percentage ☐%

Do your workings on this page

Mark to %	
0	0%
1	17%
2	33%
3	50%
4	67%
5	83%
6	100%

Daily Test 25

1) Which of these sets of numbers contains all square numbers?

A **81, 63, 36**
B **63, 25, 16**
C **121, 64, 49**
D **90, 81, 49**
E **144, 99, 810**

_____

2) The Venn diagram below shows how many children in Mrs Chandler's class like baked beans, peas or both.

3 children like neither. There are **28** children in the class. Some numbers are missing from the diagram.

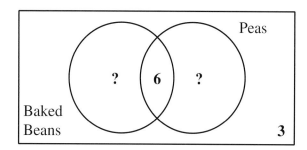

If **19** children like baked beans, how many children in the class like peas?

_____

3) Find the missing number so that the equation balances.

$$9 \times 5 + 19 = 24 \div 3 \times \underline{\quad}$$

4) What is the missing number on this grid?

24	37	50
50	63	76
63	76	

_____

5) Look at the diagram below:

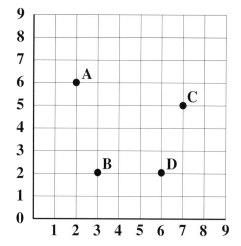

What are the co-ordinates of the points at letter **A** and letter **D**?

A: (___ , ___)

D: (___ , ___)

6) There are **15** fish fingers in a jumbo packet.

How many packets can be filled with **645** fish fingers?

_____

Score [ ] Percentage [ ] %

Do your workings on this page

Mark to %	
0	0%
1	17%
2	33%
3	50%
4	67%
5	83%
6	100%

Daily Test 26

1) Three corners of a square have the co-ordinates (**12**, **3**), (**6**, **9**) and (**6**, **3**).

   What are the co-ordinates of the fourth corner?

   (_____ , _____)

3) What is the total area of the parallelogram?

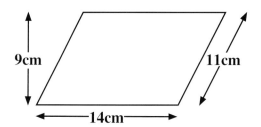

2) Which one of these shapes has twice as many acute angles as obtuse angles?

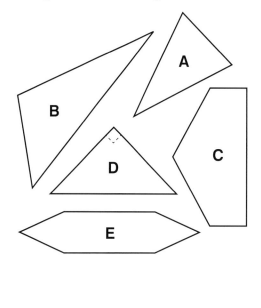

4)

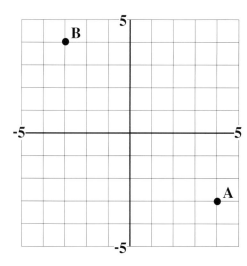

What are the co-ordinates of **A** and **B**?

	A	**B**
A	(**-4**, **3**)	(**3**, **-4**)
B	(**4**, **-3**)	(**-3**, **4**)
C	(**-3**, **4**)	(**3**, **-4**)
D	(**4**, **-3**)	(**-4**, **3**)
E	(**-3**, **4**)	(**4**, **-3**)

5) What is **90.984949** to 3 decimal places?

   _____

6) Complete the following sequence:

   3, **7**, **15**, **31**, **63**, _____

Score [   ]   Percentage [   ] %

Do your workings on this page

Mark to %	
0	0%
1	17%
2	33%
3	50%
4	67%
5	83%
6	100%

Daily Test 27

1) All the columns, rows and diagonals add up to **48**.

   What is the value of **Z**?

	Z	15
17		13

_____

---

2) Roger places **12** balls into a black bag. **Five** are yellow, **three** are green and **four** are blue.

   He takes **two** balls at random from the bag and places them on the table. Both balls are yellow.

   What is the chance that the next ball out of the bag will be another yellow one?

   A $\frac{1}{5}$ B $\frac{5}{12}$ C $\frac{3}{10}$ D $\frac{2}{5}$ E $\frac{1}{4}$

   _____

3) Johnnie and Yvonne take the bus home from school every weekday during the winter.

   Yvonne pays **55p** a day to ride on the bus. Johnnie pays an extra **30p** a day because he travels five stops further than Yvonne.

   How much does it cost them altogether to go home on the bus for **two** weeks?

   _____

---

4) Which one of these nets is the only one that will fold to form a triangular prism?

   A 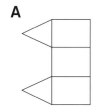   **B** 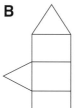   **C**   **D** 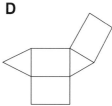   **E**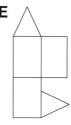

   _____

---

5) Which of the following numbers has a value closest to **50**?

   A **50.019**
   B **49.909**
   C **49.982**
   D **50.101**
   E **49.899**

   _____

6) Mrs Thomas buys **nine 5** litre bottles of spring water from the supermarket.

   Approximately how much do they weigh altogether?

   Give the answer in kilograms.

   _____

Score [ ]   Percentage [ ]%

Do your workings on this page

Mark to %	
0	0%
1	17%
2	33%
3	50%
4	67%
5	83%
6	100%

Daily Test 28

1) Lisa, Sally, Kathryn, Gillian and Emma each bought a new top.

   Sally paid **£12.50**, Emma paid **£11.99**, Kathryn paid **£14.10**, Gillian paid **£8.49** and Lisa paid **£13.75**.

   What was the range of the prices paid? _____

---

2) Which of these shapes have exactly **4** lines of symmetry?

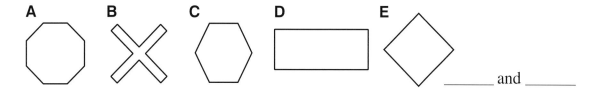

      A   **B**   **C**   **D**   **E**

   _____ and _____

---

3) Bert's aunt takes Bert and his three friends, Bill, Bob and Ben, on a steam railway trip to Scotland and back.

   It costs **£68.00** for adults. Children's tickets are half price.

   Bert's aunt has a voucher which gives them an extra **50%** off the cost of the trip.

   How much did the trip cost Bert's aunt altogether? _____

---

4) Mr Jupitus, the head teacher, went to the local shop to buy some sausages for the school summer barbecue.
   In the shop there were five different packs at five different prices:

   A Big Bangers   **£6.00** / pack of **20**
   B Vernon's Veggies   **£2.40** / pack of **6**
   C Lincolnshire Sausages **£3.65** / pack of **10**
   D Sausage Supreme   **£10.00** / pack of **25**
   E Organic Specials   **£8.00** / pack of **16**

   Which pack contains sausages at the lowest individual price? _____

6) If **7g – 19 = 79**, what is the value of **g**? _____

5) Kurt, Billy, Shannon and Eloise all collected money for charity by taking part in a sponsored silence.

   Between them they collected **£240**. They drew a pie chart to show how much each of them had collected.

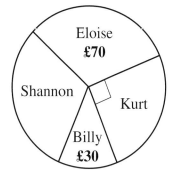

   How much did Shannon collect? _____

Score [ ] **Percentage** [ ] **%**

Do your workings on this page

Mark to %	
0	0%
1	17%
2	33%
3	50%
4	67%
5	83%
6	100%

Daily Test 29

1) The local stationery shop has a sale. Every item in the shop is reduced by **30%**.

Mrs Cartwright buys a big box of paper for her printer which normally costs **£16.50**.

How much does Mrs Cartwright have to pay for the paper in the sale?

_____

2) Look carefully at the grid below.

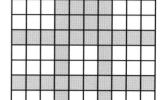

What percentage of this grid has been shaded? _____

3) Which of the figures below shows the number **six hundred and sixteen thousand and sixteen**?

A **661,616**
B **600,616**
C **616,160**
D **601,616**
E **616,016**

_____

4) This half-term Angelo has taken **ten** tables tests.

Here are his results out of **20**:

16   13   11   13   19   14   15   9   18   12

What was his mean score?

_____

5) Look at the number line below.

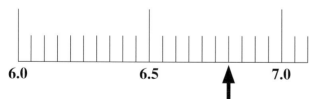

6.0   6.5   7.0

What is the value of the number that the arrow is pointing to? _____

6) Mrs Campbell's class conducted a survey in their school on the top five favourite pets.

Favourite Pets	
Dogs	☐☐☐☐■■■
Hamsters / Mice	☐☐■
Fish	☐■■■■
Cats	☐☐☐☐☐■■
Rabbits	☐☐☐☐■■■■■

Key:

☐ **5** children

■ **1** child

How many children listed rabbits as their favourite pet? _____

Score ☐ Percentage ☐ %

Do your workings on this page

Mark	to %
0	0%
1	17%
2	33%
3	50%
4	67%
5	83%
6	100%

Daily Test 30

1) What fraction of a day is **15** hours?

   Write the answer in its lowest possible terms.

   _____

2) The product of two numbers is **60**. The difference between the two numbers is **11**.

   What are the two numbers?

   _____ and _____

3) Look carefully at the graph.

   What is the rule that governs the plotting of Line A?

   A $x = 2y + 2$
   B $x = y + 1$
   C $2x = y \div 2$
   D $x \div 2 = y$
   E $x + 2 = 2y$

   _____

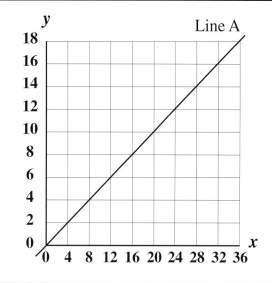

4) In a shop there are **850** DVDs.
   275 are sold to customers over the counter.
   123 are sold on the internet.

   How many DVDs remain unsold?

   _____

5) This is a floor plan of the local supermarket.

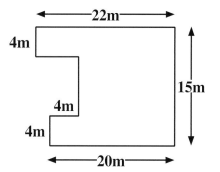

   What is the total perimeter of the floor? _____

6) Augusta is flying to Vancouver in Canada for a holiday with her family.

   There is a time difference between the United Kingdom and Vancouver. Vancouver is **8** hours behind Augusta's home in London.

   It takes $9\frac{1}{2}$ hours to fly from London to Vancouver.

   If Augusta's plane leaves London at midday, what will the time be in Vancouver when her plane lands? _____
   (Remember to state am or pm.)

 Score [ ] Percentage [%]

Do your workings on this page

Mark to %	
0	0%
1	17%
2	33%
3	50%
4	67%
5	83%
6	100%

Daily Test 31

1) What is the missing number on this grid?

101	86	71
86	71	56
71	56	

_____

2) Look at the diagram below:

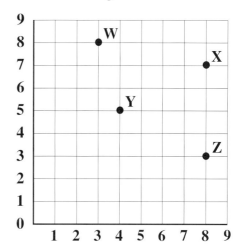

What are the co-ordinates of the points at letter **Y** and letter **X**?

Y: (___ , ___)

X: (___ , ___)

3) Jenna's cousin is now **3** times as old as Jenna was **5** years ago.

If Jenna's cousin is **24**, how old is Jenna?

_____

5) Look at the Venn diagram below. It shows how many children in Mr Bunting's class play chess, draughts or both. **5** children play neither. There are **33** children in the class.

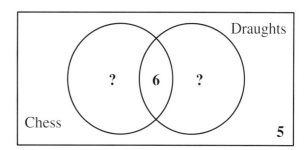

If **25** children play chess, how many children in the class play draughts in total?

_____

4) Which of these sets of numbers contains no square numbers?

A **46 49 72**
B **16 36 56**
C **36 49 144**
D **72 120 121**
E **21 45 90**

_____

6) Find the missing number so that the equation balances:

66 ÷ 11 × 8 = 120 ÷ 5 + _____

Score [ ] Percentage [ ]%

Do your workings on this page

Mark to %	
0	0%
1	17%
2	33%
3	50%
4	67%
5	83%
6	100%

Daily Test 32

1) Mrs Jennings has been collecting for charity.
   She has collected lots of money in her tin. In the last four days she has collected
   £12.25, **£13.55**, **£9.65** and **£11.48**.

   How much has she collected in total? _____

2) In this diagram, **1** small square represents **1cm²**.

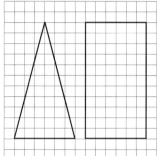

   What is the difference between the area of the rectangle and the area of the triangle?

   A **18cm²**
   B **33cm²**
   C **26cm²**
   D **22cm²**
   E **36cm²** _____

3) Miranda has drawn a plan of a football pitch. She has used a scale of **1cm** to **6m**.

   On her plan the side of the pitch measures **12cm**.

   What is the actual length of the football pitch? _____

4) Sam has **eight** 50 pence pieces, **six** 20 pence pieces, **one** 10 pence piece and **three** 5 pence pieces in her pocket.

   How much money does she have in total? _____

5) This is a map of part of St John's school. Find the way from the Head's Office to the Library using a set of instructions.

   Key:
   FD means forward, **RT** means turn right **90°** and **LT** means turn left **90°**.

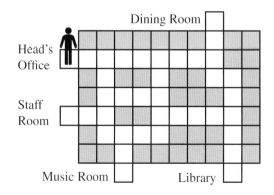

   Which of these sets of instructions is the correct one?

   A FD 5, RT, FD 3, RT, FD 4, RT, FD 3.
   B FD 8 , LT, FD 5, LT, FD 2, RT, FD 6.
   C FD 2, LT, FD 3, RT, FD 5, RT, FD 3.
   D FD 5, RT, FD 3, LT, FD 4, RT, FD 3.
   E FD 2, RT, FD 3, LT, FD 8, RT, FD 6.
   _____

6) There are **25** erasers in a box.

   How many boxes can be filled with **425** erasers? _____

Score [   ]   Percentage [%]

Do your workings on this page

Mark to %	
0	0%
1	17%
2	33%
3	50%
4	67%
5	83%
6	100%

Daily Test 33

1) When folded this net makes a box.

   If the side of each small square is **5cm**, what will be the total surface area of the box?

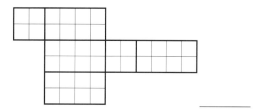

_____

---

2) There are **50** children on a bus; **35** girls and **15** boys.
   One child's name is chosen at random to collect the tickets.

   What is the chance that the child will be a girl?

   (Write the answer as a fraction in its lowest terms.)   _____

3) If the perimeter of a rectangle is **18cm**, which of the following could be the area of that rectangle?

   A **18cm²**
   B **10cm²**
   C **24cm²**
   D **36cm²**
   E **30cm²**   _____

---

4) This is Geoff's function machine. What number did he start with?

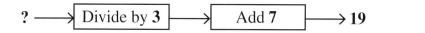

? ⟶ | Divide by **3** | ⟶ | Add **7** | ⟶ **19**

_____

---

5) Roger, Simon, Kamran, James and Rahul all stood for election to become captain of the cricket club.

   240 people voted for which person they wanted to be captain. The results of the number of votes cast are shown in this pie chart.

   How many votes did Kamran receive?

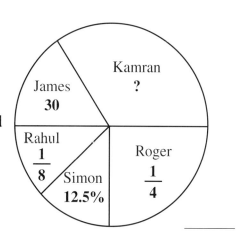

_____

---

6) How would **a quarter to seven in the evening** be shown on a 24-hour clock?

_____

Score ☐ Percentage ☐ **%**

Do your workings on this page

Mark to %	
0	0%
1	17%
2	33%
3	50%
4	67%
5	83%
6	100%

Daily Test 34

1) The ratio of boys to girls in a music class is **4 : 5**.

   If there are **36** children in the class, how many of them are boys? _____

2) This spinner has an equal chance of landing on any of the numbers.

   What is the chance that it will come to rest on a number that is a prime number?

   Write the answer as a fraction in its lowest possible terms.

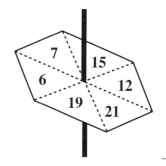

   _____

3) The hands of the classroom clock show the time **9 o'clock**.

   What is the size of the reflex angle between the hour hand and the minute hand? _____

4) Five children collected aluminium cans for the school recycling drive. The bar chart below shows how many cans each of the children collected.

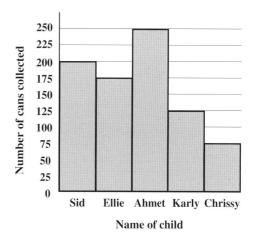

   How many more cans were collected by Ahmet than by Chrissy? _____

5) Miss Jennings takes five pupils to see a free exhibition in London.
   Train tickets cost **£6.80** per child.
   The price of an adult's ticket is **£3.20** more than that of a child.

   How much does it cost in total to visit the exhibition? _____

6) How many faces would there be on a shape made by two identical cubes that have been stuck together, face-to-face? _____

Score [   ] Percentage [%]

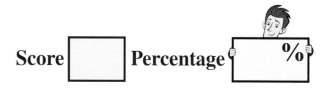

Do your workings on this page

Mark to %	
0	0%
1	17%
2	33%
3	50%
4	67%
5	83%
6	100%

Daily Test 35

1) Jenny places some weights on an electronic scale.
   She needs to make a total of **4.250kg**.

   Which two weights should she choose
   to make up the weight to the correct
   amount?

   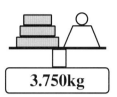

   3.750kg

   A **375g** B **175g** C **225g** D **125g** E **350g**   ____ and ____

---

2) Chris and Vinny go to an after school club each weekday during the spring term.

   They have to pay **75p** a day each to attend.
   They also pay an extra **35p** a day to have a drink.

   How much will it cost the pair of them to go to the after school
   club for **one** week?   _____

Thorpe Culvert   Wainfleet   Havenhouse   Skegness

3) A train ran between Thorpe Culvert and Skegness railway stations.
   There were **57** passengers on the train when it left Thorpe Culvert.
   8 people got out at Wainfleet and **19** people got on.
   23 left the train at Havenhouse whilst **29** got on.

   How many people were on the train at when it arrived at Skegness?   _____

---

4) Mum gives **y** pounds pocket
   money to John each week
   and **x** pounds pocket money
   to Jenny each month.

   How much does mum give
   them in total in a year?

   A $12x + 7y$
   B $52x + 12y$
   C $7x + 12y$
   D $12x + 52y$
   E $10x + 12y$ _____

5) Look at the shape below.
   The area of the shape that is coloured
   black is **27cm²**.

   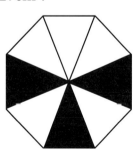

   What area of the
   shape is unshaded?   _____

---

6) Mr Frederick bought **13,500** printed shopping bags for his customers at the
   local supermarket. They come packed in boxes of **45**.

   How many boxes of shopping bags did Mr Frederick buy?   _____

Score [   ]   Percentage [%]

Do your workings on this page

Mark to %	
0	0%
1	17%
2	33%
3	50%
4	67%
5	83%
6	100%

Daily Test 36

1) Jack Joiner, the carpenter, bought a box of **1,000** screws.
He used **239** screws on one job.
366 were used on his next job.

How many screws remained unused? _____

2) This is a plan of the patio Mrs Jenkins wants to build.

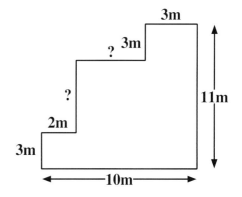

How many **1m²** paving slabs does she need to cover the patio?

_____

3) Yasmeen is flying to Karachi in Pakistan to visit her grandparents.
There is a time difference between the United Kingdom and Karachi. Yasmeen's home in Birmingham is **5** hours behind her grandparents' home in Karachi.

It takes **8** hours to fly from Birmingham to Karachi.

If Yasmeen's plane leaves Birmingham at **8am**, what will the time be in Karachi when her plane touches down? (Remember to state am or pm.)

_____

4) What fraction of a day is **4** hours?

Write the answer in its lowest possible terms.

_____

5) The product of two numbers is **48**.
The difference between the two numbers is **13**.

What are the two numbers? _____ and _____

6) Look carefully at the graph below.

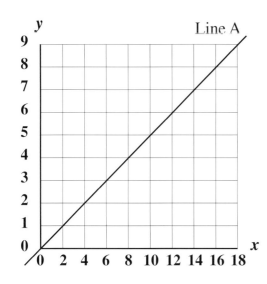

What is the rule that governs the plotting of Line A?

A $x + 1 = y$
B $x = y - 2$
C $x = 2y$
D $x - 2 = y$
E $2y - x = y$

_____

Score [ ]   Percentage [ ] %

Do your workings on this page

Mark to %	
0	0%
1	17%
2	33%
3	50%
4	67%
5	83%
6	100%

Daily Test 37

1) This half-term Nicola has taken nine spelling tests. Here are her results out of **20**:

14 11 14 11 8 16 15 18 10

What was her mean score?

_____

2) Look at the number line below.

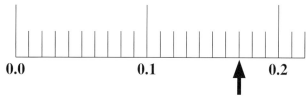

0.0   0.1   0.2

What is the value of the number that the arrow is pointing to?

_____

3) Mrs Campbell's class conducted a survey in their school on favourite types of music.

Favourite Types of Music	
Heavy Metal	□□■
Brass Band	□■■
Hip Hop	□□■■■
Classical	■■■
Pop	□□□□■■

Key:

□ **4** children

■ **1** child

How many more children liked Pop than Hip Hop?

_____

4) The local mobile phone shop has a sale.
Every item in the shop is reduced by **25%**.
Georgie buys a new telephone which normally costs **£90.00**.

How much does Georgie have to pay for the phone in the sale?   _____

5) Look carefully at the grid below.

What percentage of this grid is coloured white?

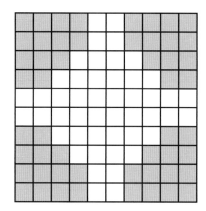

_____

6) Which of the figures below shows the number **seventy-seven thousand and seventy-seven**?

A **770,077**
B **77,770**
C **77,077**
D **707,077**
E **7,777**

_____

Score [ ] Percentage [ ] %

Do your workings on this page

Mark to %	
0	0%
1	17%
2	33%
3	50%
4	67%
5	83%
6	100%

Daily Test 38

1) Below are some prices from the local bakery.

Vanilla Slice	80p each
Raspberry Jam Doughnut	50p each
Chocolate Éclair	90p each
Fairy Cake	30p each
Individual Bakewell Tart	45p each

How much would it cost to buy **4** fairy cakes, **2** chocolate éclairs and **1** each of the remaining **three** types of cake?

A **£3.75**

B **£4.75**

C **£4.10**

D **£4.45**

E **£5.05**

_____

2) The children in all the local schools took part in a vote to find out which was their favourite pop group. The results are shown in this pie chart.

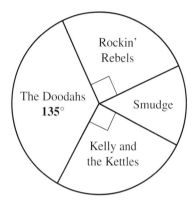

In all, **2,000** children took part in the vote.

How many votes did Smudge receive?

_____

3) If **6t – 12 = 60**, what is the value of *t*?

_____

4) Juanita, Shahnaz, Laura, Sally and Joanie each bought a CD from the local supermarket.

Joanie paid **£8.49**, Shahnaz paid **£9.99**, Laura paid **£5.69**, Juanita paid **£10.99** and Sally paid **£7.89**.

What was the range of the prices paid?

_____

5) Which of these shapes has a rotational symmetry of order **2**?

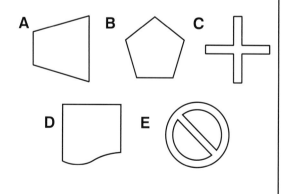

_____

6) Mervyn's grandma takes Mervyn and his three friends to Frumton zoo for a treat.

It costs **£8.00** for adults and **£4.00** each for children. Each child also bought an ice cream and Mervyn's grandma had a cup of coffee.

Ice creams are **£1.50** each and a cup of coffee cost **£1.20**.

How much did the trip cost Mervyn's grandma altogether?

_____

Score [ ] Percentage [ ] %

Do your workings on this page

Mark to %	
0	0%
1	17%
2	33%
3	50%
4	67%
5	83%
6	100%

Daily Test 39

1) All the columns, rows and diagonals add up to **39**.

18		12
14	**X**	

What number should replace the letter **X**? _____

2) Rebecca places **13** balls into a black bag. **Five** are green, **four** are red and **four** are blue.

She takes **one** ball at random from the bag and places it on the table. It is red.

What is the chance that the next ball out of the bag will be blue?

A $\frac{1}{4}$ B $\frac{4}{13}$ C $\frac{4}{9}$ D $\frac{5}{12}$ E $\frac{1}{3}$

_____

3) Sam's mum buys **eight 2** litre bottles of lemonade and **six 1** litre bottles of cola from the supermarket.

Approximately how much do the bottles weigh altogether?

Give the answer in kilograms. _____

4) Look at the nets below.
Which of these nets will fold to form a cuboid?

A   B   C   D 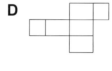   E

_____ and _____

5) Three brothers, Basil, Charlie and Nikolas, go to a football training camp each weekday morning during the holidays. They each have to pay **£1.10** a day to attend. They have to pay extra for drinks. Charlie buys **one** each day, whilst the others have **two**. The drinks cost **50p**.

How much will it cost altogether for the three of them to attend football training for **one** week?

_____

6) Look at the numbers below.

Which of the following numbers has a value closest to **15**?

A **14.909**
B **15.101**
C **14.190**
D **14.995**
E **14.899**

_____

Score [   ]   Percentage [%]

Do your workings on this page

Mark to %	
0	0%
1	17%
2	33%
3	50%
4	67%
5	83%
6	100%

Daily Test 40

1) Three corners of a rectangle have the co-ordinates (**4**, **9**), (**9**, **9**) and (**4**, **2**).

   What are the co-ordinates of the fourth corner? (____ , ____)

---

2) Look at the shapes below.

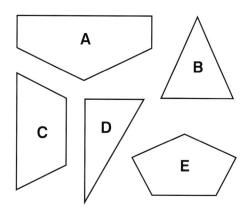

   Which one of these shapes
   contains two obtuse angles? _____

3) What is the total area of this
   trapezium?

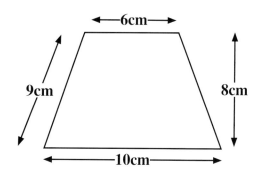

   _____

4) Look at the graph.

   What are the co-ordinates of **E** and **F**?

	E	**F**
A	(**2**, **-3**)	(**3**, **-4**)
B	(**-3**, **-2**)	(**3**, **-4**)
C	(**3**, **-2**)	(**-4**, **3**)
D	(**-3**, **2**)	(**4**, **-3**)
E	(**-2**, **3**)	(**4**, **3**)

   _____

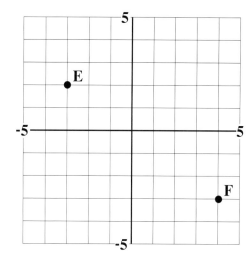

---

5) What is **19.94865** to 2 decimal places?

   _____

6) Complete the following sequence:

   12, **9**, **18**, **15**, **30**, **27**, _____

Score ☐ Percentage ☐ %

Multiple-choice Answer Sheet

11+ Maths Year 5-7 Testbook 3

Test 1

1	2	3	4	5	6
109 ▭	F: (6, 2) G: (7, 3) ▭	18 ▭	A ▭	14 ▭	12 ▭
103 ▭	F: (2, 6) G: (7, 3) ▭	20 ▭	B ▭	21 ▭	8 ▭
108 ▭	F: (3, 7) G: (2, 6) ▭	24 ▭	C ▭	18 ▭	11 ▭
115 ▭	F: (6, 2) G: (3, 7) ▭	19 ▭	D ▭	15 ▭	15 ▭
113 ▭	F: (7, 3) G: (6, 2) ▭	21 ▭	E ▭	22 ▭	13 ▭

Test 2

1	2	3	4	5	6
£3.75 ▭	A ▭	25 ▭	£14.90 ▭	$45 ▭	3.40pm ▭
£2.95 ▭	B ▭	23 ▭	£10.65 ▭	$42 ▭	3.35pm ▭
£2.65 ▭	C ▭	21 ▭	£14.95 ▭	$30 ▭	3.25am ▭
£2.55 ▭	D ▭	24 ▭	£11.85 ▭	$55 ▭	3.30pm ▭
£2.75 ▭	E ▭	30 ▭	£12.75 ▭	$50 ▭	15:45 ▭

Test 3

1	2	3	4	5	6
70cm^2 ▭	$3/4$ ▭	15 ▭	100 ▭	80 ▭	22:30 ▭
180cm^2 ▭	$1/2$ ▭	10 ▭	80 ▭	66 ▭	10:30 ▭
160cm^2 ▭	$5/9$ ▭	30 ▭	140 ▭	62 ▭	20:30 ▭
170cm^2 ▭	$5/8$ ▭	50 ▭	130 ▭	70 ▭	21:30 ▭
80cm^2 ▭	$7/16$ ▭	45 ▭	60 ▭	84 ▭	21:00 ▭

Test 4

1	2	3	4	5	6
130 ▭	£24.75 ▭	10 ▭	0.75kg ▭	$2/3$ ▭	175° ▭
115 ▭	£22.25 ▭	5 ▭	0.8kg ▭	$3/4$ ▭	180° ▭
110 ▭	£20.50 ▭	6 ▭	1.5kg ▭	$1/3$ ▭	160° ▭
125 ▭	£21.75 ▭	8 ▭	1kg ▭	$1/4$ ▭	170° ▭
105 ▭	£23.75 ▭	7 ▭	0.95kg ▭	$1/8$ ▭	150° ▭

Test 5

1	2	3	4	5	6
A & B ▭	£7.30 ▭	61 ▭	A ▭	48cm^2 ▭	25 ▭
A & D ▭	£10.00 ▭	68 ▭	B ▭	64cm^2 ▭	21 ▭
C & E ▭	£9.50 ▭	58 ▭	C ▭	56cm^2 ▭	17 ▭
B & D ▭	£9.00 ▭	43 ▭	D ▭	40cm^2 ▭	18 ▭
D & E ▭	£8.50 ▭	47 ▭	E ▭	52cm^2 ▭	22 ▭

Test 6

1	2	3	4	5	6
421ℓ ▭	75m ▭	11am ▭	$3/8$ ▭	7 and 11 ▭	A ▭
389ℓ ▭	68m ▭	9am ▭	$3/4$ ▭	5 and 11 ▭	B ▭
467ℓ ▭	54m ▭	12pm ▭	$1/3$ ▭	6 and 13 ▭	C ▭
449ℓ ▭	180m ▭	2pm ▭	$2/3$ ▭	7 and 13 ▭	D ▭
437ℓ ▭	110m ▭	7pm ▭	$1/8$ ▭	6 and 12 ▭	E ▭

Test 7

1	2	3	4	5	6
£20.00 ▭	68% ▭	A ▭	12 ▭	6.8 ▭	24 ▭
£14.00 ▭	62% ▭	B ▭	16 ▭	7.4 ▭	15 ▭
£21.00 ▭	72% ▭	C ▭	14 ▭	6.9 ▭	20 ▭
£18.00 ▭	60% ▭	D ▭	15 ▭	6.7 ▭	21 ▭
£23.00 ▭	70% ▭	E ▭	13 ▭	8.1 ▭	28 ▭

Multiple-choice Answer Sheet

11+ Maths Year 5-7 Testbook 3

Test 8

1	2	3	4	5	6
A ▭	30 ▭	4 ▭	£4.44 ▭	A ▭	£29.35 ▭
B ▭	25 ▭	6 ▭	£4.54 ▭	B ▭	£34.00 ▭
C ▭	20 ▭	8 ▭	£4.96 ▭	C ▭	£31.25 ▭
D ▭	15 ▭	5 ▭	£4.84 ▭	D ▭	£35.60 ▭
E ▭	24 ▭	3 ▭	£5.16 ▭	E ▭	£29.75 ▭

Test 9

1	2	3	4	5	6
A ▭	£9.50 ▭	9kg ▭	16 ▭	A ▭	9.995 ▭
B ▭	£8.30 ▭	10kg ▭	19 ▭	B ▭	10.899 ▭
C ▭	£11.00 ▭	12kg ▭	21 ▭	C ▭	10.190 ▭
D ▭	£9.80 ▭	11kg ▭	18 ▭	D ▭	9.909 ▭
E ▭	£10.30 ▭	8kg ▭	17 ▭	E ▭	9.992 ▭

Test 10

1	2	3	4	5	6
(6, 1) ▭	A ▭	30cm^2 ▭	A ▭	10.75 ▭	85 ▭
(2, 1) ▭	B ▭	45cm^2 ▭	B ▭	10.757 ▭	70 ▭
(2, 2) ▭	C ▭	11cm^2 ▭	C ▭	10.76 ▭	80 ▭
(6, 2) ▭	D ▭	15cm^2 ▭	D ▭	10.756 ▭	75 ▭
(2, 6) ▭	E ▭	20cm^2 ▭	E ▭	10.8 ▭	90 ▭

Test 11

1	2	3	4	5	6
A ▭	35cm^2 ▭	21 ▭	D & E ▭	£16.50 ▭	52 ▭
B ▭	21cm^2 ▭	30 ▭	A & C ▭	£6.90 ▭	54 ▭
C ▭	30cm^2 ▭	25 ▭	B & D ▭	£12.90 ▭	48 ▭
D ▭	56cm^2 ▭	22 ▭	C & E ▭	£10.50 ▭	49 ▭
E ▭	28cm^2 ▭	19 ▭	A & D ▭	£21.00 ▭	57 ▭

Test 12

1	2	3	4	5	6
500 grams ▭	$\frac{1}{6}$ ▭	120° ▭	100 ▭	£30.00 ▭	14 ▭
800 grams ▭	$\frac{1}{2}$ ▭	240° ▭	105 ▭	£37.50 ▭	10 ▭
900 grams ▭	$\frac{2}{3}$ ▭	180° ▭	120 ▭	£34.00 ▭	11 ▭
750 grams ▭	$\frac{5}{6}$ ▭	130° ▭	150 ▭	£32.00 ▭	20 ▭
1,000 grams ▭	$\frac{3}{5}$ ▭	200° ▭	125 ▭	£32.75 ▭	12 ▭

Test 13

1	2	3	4	5	6
80 ▭	84 ▭	23:30 ▭	240cm^2 ▭	$\frac{4}{5}$ ▭	90 ▭
75 ▭	88 ▭	11:30 ▭	160cm^2 ▭	$\frac{2}{3}$ ▭	45 ▭
60 ▭	66 ▭	11.30pm ▭	140cm^2 ▭	$\frac{7}{16}$ ▭	75 ▭
70 ▭	72 ▭	22:30 ▭	165cm^2 ▭	$\frac{19}{32}$ ▭	35 ▭
65 ▭	82 ▭	21:30 ▭	200cm^2 ▭	$\frac{4}{9}$ ▭	40 ▭

Test 14

1	2	3	4	5	6
£33.20 ▭	£36 ▭	3.30pm ▭	£3.50 ▭	A ▭	25 ▭
£30.29 ▭	£45 ▭	3.20pm ▭	£3.30 ▭	B ▭	27 ▭
£31.20 ▭	£41 ▭	3.15pm ▭	£3.25 ▭	C ▭	29 ▭
£33.49 ▭	£38 ▭	3.40pm ▭	£3.35 ▭	D ▭	28 ▭
£32.71 ▭	£40 ▭	3.45pm ▭	£3.10 ▭	E ▭	32 ▭

Multiple-choice Answer Sheet

11+ Maths Year 5-7 Testbook 3

Test 15

1
- A ☐
- B ☐
- C ☐
- D ☐
- E ☐

2
- 16 ☐
- 9 ☐
- 12 ☐
- 11 ☐
- 5 ☐

3
- 29 ☐
- 30 ☐
- 27 ☐
- 28 ☐
- 32 ☐

4
- 64 ☐
- 65 ☐
- 52 ☐
- 39 ☐
- 55 ☐

5
- W: (3, 2) X: (6, 5) ☐
- W: (6, 5) X: (2, 3) ☐
- W: (6, 5) X: (3, 2) ☐
- W: (3, 2) X: (5, 6) ☐
- W: (5, 6) X: (2, 3) ☐

6
- 32 ☐
- 26 ☐
- 22 ☐
- 31 ☐
- 18 ☐

Test 16

1
- A ☐
- B ☐
- C ☐
- D ☐
- E ☐

2
- 59.01 ☐
- 59.09 ☐
- 59.1 ☐
- 59.0 ☐
- 59.11 ☐

3
- 51 ☐
- 48 ☐
- 47 ☐
- 49 ☐
- 52 ☐

4
- (9, 2) ☐
- (5, 9) ☐
- (2, 9) ☐
- (5, 2) ☐
- (2, 5) ☐

5
- A ☐
- B ☐
- C ☐
- D ☐
- E ☐

6
- $36cm^2$ ☐
- $48cm^2$ ☐
- $28cm^2$ ☐
- $24cm^2$ ☐
- $38cm^2$ ☐

Test 17

1
- 18 ☐
- 24 ☐
- 17 ☐
- 19 ☐
- 22 ☐

2
- A ☐
- B ☐
- C ☐
- D ☐
- E ☐

3
- £20.00 ☐
- £10.00 ☐
- £18.00 ☐
- £14.00 ☐
- £16.00 ☐

4
- A ☐
- B ☐
- C ☐
- D ☐
- E ☐

5
- A ☐
- B ☐
- C ☐
- D ☐
- E ☐

6
- 6kg ☐
- 24kg ☐
- 12kg ☐
- 3kg ☐
- 30kg ☐

Test 18

1
- £7.35 ☐
- £6.95 ☐
- £25.15 ☐
- £11.45 ☐
- £7.95 ☐

2
- A ☐
- B ☐
- C ☐
- D ☐
- E ☐

3
- £106 ☐
- £158 ☐
- £112 ☐
- £138 ☐
- £125 ☐

4
- A ☐
- B ☐
- C ☐
- D ☐
- E ☐

5
- £150 ☐
- £120 ☐
- £175 ☐
- £145 ☐
- £160 ☐

6
- 6 ☐
- 8 ☐
- 9 ☐
- 4 ☐
- 7 ☐

Test 19

1
- 19 ☐
- 14 ☐
- 13 ☐
- 15 ☐
- 17 ☐

2
- 1.14 ☐
- 1.40 ☐
- 1.04 ☐
- 1.10 ☐
- 1.24 ☐

3
- 18 ☐
- 13 ☐
- 19 ☐
- 12 ☐
- 17 ☐

4
- £300 ☐
- £270 ☐
- £250 ☐
- £335 ☐
- £245 ☐

5
- 80% ☐
- 75% ☐
- 60% ☐
- 70% ☐
- 85% ☐

6
- A ☐
- B ☐
- C ☐
- D ☐
- E ☐

Test 20

1
- $5/8$ ☐
- $2/3$ ☐
- $3/4$ ☐
- $7/8$ ☐
- $7/9$ ☐

2
- 14 and 2 ☐
- 16 and 4 ☐
- 15 and 3 ☐
- 13 and 2 ☐
- 12 and 2 ☐

3
- A ☐
- B ☐
- C ☐
- D ☐
- E ☐

4
- 539 ☐
- 495 ☐
- 449 ☐
- 519 ☐
- 605 ☐

5
- 26m ☐
- 52m ☐
- 84m ☐
- 120m ☐
- 165m ☐

6
- 3pm ☐
- 2pm ☐
- 11am ☐
- 5pm ☐
- 7pm ☐

Test 21

1
- B & C ☐
- A & E ☐
- C & E ☐
- B & D ☐
- A & D ☐

2
- £37.00 ☐
- £33.00 ☐
- £42.00 ☐
- £21.00 ☐
- £25.80 ☐

3
- 54 ☐
- 52 ☐
- 51 ☐
- 59 ☐
- 57 ☐

4
- A ☐
- B ☐
- C ☐
- D ☐
- E ☐

5
- $75cm^2$ ☐
- $105cm^2$ ☐
- $95cm^2$ ☐
- $80cm^2$ ☐
- $100cm^2$ ☐

6
- 18 ☐
- 20 ☐
- 15 ☐
- 22 ☐
- 12 ☐

Multiple-choice Answer Sheet

11+ Maths Year 5-7 Testbook 3

Test 22

1	2	3	4	5	6
500g	$^2/_6$	40°	100	£33.00	15
350g	$^5/_6$	230°	110	£38.50	24
400g	$^1/_3$	60°	120	£44.00	27
450g	$^2/_3$	80°	150	£27.50	18
300g	$^1/_2$	300°	90	£40.50	21

Test 23

1	2	3	4	5	6
48	36	02:15	2,500cm³	$^2/_3$	16
72	54	01.45pm	1,250cm³	$^5/_8$	20
120	40	13:45	250cm³	$^1/_2$	18
80	45	1:45	500cm³	$^2/_6$	25
150	30	13.45pm	125cm³	$^3/_8$	10

Test 24

1	2	3	4	5	6
£3.65	A	34	£37.90	£35	12.10am
£4.15	B	38	£38.50	£30	11.50am
£3.95	C	40	£41.20	£45	13.30pm
£3.85	D	36	£40.00	£50	12.10pm
£3.75	E	32	£36.50	£40	11.30pm

Test 25

1	2	3	4	5	6
A	15	8	99	A: (6, 2) D: (2, 6)	50
B	9	6	79	A: (6, 2) D: (6, 2)	43
C	10	4	86	A: (7, 3) D: (2, 6)	39
D	12	9	89	A: (2, 6) D: (6, 2)	45
E	6	12	96	A: (3, 7) D: (6, 2)	48

Test 26

1	2	3	4	5	6
(9, 12)	A	126cm²	A	90.984	91
(3, 12)	B	154cm²	B	90.980	118
(12, 9)	C	140cm²	C	91.000	99
(6, 12)	D	99cm²	D	90.985	94
(3, 6)	E	160cm²	E	90.990	127

Test 27

1	2	3	4	5	6
18	A	£20.00	A	A	36kg
17	B	£10.00	B	B	45kg
14	C	£18.00	C	C	25kg
19	D	£14.00	D	D	14kg
16	E	£16.00	E	E	30kg

Test 28

1	2	3	4	5	6
£5.26	C & E	£102	A	£75	16
£4.80	A & D	£85	B	£60	18
£5.61	B & E	£204	C	£80	12
£10.60	A & B	£170	D	£90	15
£9.60	D & E	£51	E	£70	14

Multiple-choice Answer Sheet

11+ Maths Year 5-7 Testbook 3

Test 29

1
- £13.00
- £11.85
- £12.50
- £11.55
- £12.35

2
- 44%
- 56%
- 42%
- 38%
- 58%

3
- A
- B
- C
- D
- E

4
- 16
- 14
- 13
- 15
- 12

5
- 6.70
- 6.65
- 6.80
- 6.75
- 6.60

6
- 20
- 44
- 18
- 21
- 24

Test 30

1
- $3/5$
- $7/12$
- $2/3$
- $5/8$
- $4/6$

2
- 13 and 2
- 15 and 4
- 14 and 3
- 16 and 5
- 17 and 6

3
- A
- B
- C
- D
- E

4
- 498
- 452
- 423
- 398
- 352

5
- 82m
- 69m
- 84m
- 120m
- 74m

6
- 10.30am
- 3.00pm
- 10.30pm
- 1.30pm
- 3.00am

Test 31

1
- 86
- 39
- 41
- 44
- 38

2
- X: (5, 4) Y: (7, 8)
- X: (8, 7) Y: (4, 5)
- X: (7, 8) Y: (5, 4)
- X: (8, 7) Y: (5, 4)
- X: (4, 5) Y: (8, 7)

3
- 11
- 15
- 12
- 10
- 13

4
- A
- B
- C
- D
- E

5
- 9
- 8
- 14
- 8
- 12

6
- 32
- 24
- 30
- 26
- 20

Test 32

1
- £45.98
- £10.65
- £14.93
- £11.85
- £46.93

2
- A
- B
- C
- D
- E

3
- 36m
- 56m
- 48m
- 72m
- 60m

4
- £5.45
- £5.30
- £4.95
- £5.95
- £5.25

5
- A
- B
- C
- D
- E

6
- 18
- 19
- 17
- 21
- 15

Test 33

1
- 750cm²
- 1,000cm²
- 720cm²
- 960cm²
- 480cm²

2
- $3/10$
- $2/3$
- $3/5$
- $4/5$
- $7/10$

3
- A
- B
- C
- D
- E

4
- 36
- 32
- 28
- 35
- 17

5
- 45
- 75
- 90
- 85
- 60

6
- 18:45
- 20:15
- 06:30
- 07:15
- 06:45

Test 34

1
- 16
- 18
- 30
- 24
- 20

2
- $1/2$
- $5/6$
- $2/3$
- $1/3$
- $2/6$

3
- 90°
- 315°
- 160°
- 270°
- 240°

4
- 125
- 175
- 150
- 225
- 200

5
- £37.20
- £22.25
- £38.40
- £44.00
- £30.40

6
- 10
- 5
- 6
- 8
- 12

Test 35

1
- A & E
- B & D
- C & E
- B & C
- A & D

2
- £7.30
- £11.00
- £9.50
- £15.40
- £9.25

3
- 61
- 74
- 82
- 16
- 68

4
- A
- B
- C
- D
- E

5
- 72cm²
- 36cm²
- 27cm²
- 63cm²
- 45cm²

6
- 25
- 300
- 200
- 30
- 350

Multiple-choice Answer Sheet

11+ Maths Year 5-7 Testbook 3

Test 36

1
- 295
- 305
- 395
- 375
- 405

2
- 79 slabs
- 110 slabs
- 96 slabs
- 73 slabs
- 100 slabs

3
- 3am
- 5pm
- 11pm
- 9pm
- 11am

4
- $\frac{1}{8}$
- $\frac{3}{12}$
- $\frac{2}{12}$
- $\frac{1}{6}$
- $\frac{2}{5}$

5
- 7 and 20
- 3 and 16
- 6 and 13
- 4 and 16
- 5 and 18

6
- A
- B
- C
- D
- E

Test 37

1
- 13
- 16
- 15
- 14
- 16

2
- 1.70
- 0.17
- 0.71
- 0.70
- 0.16

3
- 9
- 10
- 11
- 7
- 8

4
- £65.00
- £60.00
- £57.50
- £67.50
- £62.50

5
- 52%
- 38%
- 45%
- 48%
- 60%

6
- A
- B
- C
- D
- E

Test 38

1
- A
- B
- C
- D
- E

2
- 310
- 325
- 300
- 250
- 275

3
- 9
- 8
- 15
- 12
- 7

4
- £6.20
- £7.10
- £6.90
- £5.80
- £5.30

5
- A
- B
- C
- D
- E

6
- £31.20
- £29.70
- £25.70
- £35.60
- £27.20

Test 39

1
- 15
- 8
- 13
- 16
- 17

2
- A
- B
- C
- D
- E

3
- 16kg
- 20kg
- 22kg
- 18kg
- 24kg

4
- A & C
- B & D
- B & E
- A & E
- C & D

5
- £23.50
- £28.50
- £18.00
- £29.00
- £20.50

6
- A
- B
- C
- D
- E

Test 40

1
- (2, 9)
- (2, 4)
- (9, 2)
- (9, 4)
- (4, 9)

2
- A
- B
- C
- D
- E

3
- 48cm²
- 80cm²
- 72cm²
- 64cm²
- 33cm²

4
- A
- B
- C
- D
- E

5
- 19.94
- 19.948
- 19.95
- 19.940
- 19.90

6
- 24
- 54
- 57
- 60
- 58

Answers

Test 1
1) 113
2) F: (6, 2)
   G: (3, 7)
3) 20
4) D
5) 21
6) 11

Test 2
1) £2.65
2) D
3) 21
4) £14.90
5) $45
6) 3.35pm

Test 3
1) 160cm^2
2) $^5/_9$
3) 15
4) 60
5) 70
6) 22:30

Test 4
1) 125
2) £23.75
3) 5
4) 1kg
5) $^1/_3$
6) 150°

Test 5
1) A & D
2) £8.50
3) 61
4) E
5) 56cm^2
6) 21

Test 6
1) 449ℓ
2) 54m
3) 7pm
4) $^2/_3$
5) 6 & 12
6) D

Test 7
1) £21
2) 68%
3) C
4) 13
5) 7.4
6) 21

Test 8
1) C
2) 15
3) 3
4) £4.96
5) E
6) £35.60

Test 9
1) D & E
2) £9.50
3) 12kg
4) 16
5) B
6) 9.995

Test 10
1) (6, 2)
2) A
3) 15cm^2
4) D
5) 10.76
6) 75

Test 11
1) A
2) 21cm^2
3) 19
4) B & D
5) £16.50
6) 54

Test 12
1) 750g
2) $^1/_2$
3) 240°
4) 150
5) £34.00
6) 12

Test 13
1) 75
2) 72
3) 23:30
4) 200cm^2
5) $^2/_3$
6) 35

Test 14
1) £33.20
2) £40
3) 3.30pm
4) £3.10
5) D
6) 28

Test 15
1) D
2) 12
3) 27
4) 65
5) W: (6, 5)
   X: (3, 2)
6) 31

Test 16
1) B
2) 59.1
3) 52
4) (5, 2)
5) B
6) 48cm^2

Test 17
1) 22
2) A
3) £18.00
4) D
5) C
6) 30kg

Test 18
1) £7.35
2) B
3) £158.00
4) E
5) £175.00
6) 6

Test 19
1) 15
2) 1.14
3) 17
4) £270.00
5) 70%
6) C

Test 20
1) $^3/_4$
2) 15 and 3
3) A
4) 539
5) 52m
6) 2pm

Answers

Test 21
1) A and D
2) £33.00
3) 59
4) E
5) 75cm^2
6) 15

Test 22
1) 350g
2) $^2/_3$
3) 60°
4) 150ℓ
5) £38.50
6) 18

Test 23
1) 120
2) 36
3) 13:45
4) 2,500cm^3
5) $^3/_8$
6) 16

Test 24
1) £4.15
2) A
3) 34
4) £40.00
5) £40
6) 12.10pm

Test 25
1) C
2) 12
3) 8
4) 89
5) A: (2, 6)
   D: (6, 2)
6) 43 packets

Test 26
1) (12, 9)
2) B
3) 126cm^2
4) B
5) 90.985
6) 127

Test 27
1) 14
2) C
3) £14.00
4) D
5) C
6) 45kg

Test 28
1) £5.61
2) B and E
3) £102.00
4) A
5) £80.00
6) 14

Test 29
1) £11.55
2) 42%
3) E
4) 14
5) 6.8
6) 24

Test 30
1) $^5/_8$
2) 15 and 4
3) D
4) 452
5) 82m
6) 1.30pm

Test 31
1) 41
2) Y: (4, 5)
   X: (8, 7)
3) 13
4) E
5) 9
6) 24

Test 32
1) £46.93
2) B
3) 72m
4) £5.45
5) D
6) 17

Test 33
1) 1,000cm^2
2) $^7/_{10}$
3) A
4) 36
5) 90
6) 18:45

Test 34
1) 16
2) $^1/_3$
3) 270°
4) 175
5) £44.00
6) 6

Test 35
1) A and D
2) £11.00
3) 74
4) D
5) 45cm^2
6) 300

Test 36
1) 395
2) 79
3) 9.00pm
4) $^1/_6$
5) 3 and 16
6) C

Test 37
1) 13
2) 0.17
3) 7
4) £67.50
5) 48%
6) C

Test 38
1) B
2) 250
3) 12
4) £5.30
5) E
6) £31.20

Test 39
1) 17
2) E
3) 22kg
4) A and E
5) £29.00
6) D

Test 40
1) (9, 2)
2) C
3) 64cm^2
4) D
5) 19.95
6) 54

PROGRESS CHARTS

Test	Score	%
1		
2		
3		
4		
5		
6		
7		
8		
9		
10		
11		
12		
13		
14		
15		
16		
17		
18		
19		
20		

Test	Score	%
21		
22		
23		
24		
25		
26		
27		
28		
29		
30		
31		
32		
33		
34		
35		
36		
37		
38		
39		
40		

CERTIFICATE OF

ACHIEVEMENT

This certifies

_____

has successfully completed

11+ Maths
Year 5–7
TESTBOOK **3**

Overall percentage
score achieved | | **%**

Comment _____

_____

Signed _____
(teacher/parent/guardian)

Date _____